GOODNIGHT LITTLE ROCK

Written by Emily Wyatt • Illustrated by Nathaniel Dailey

Emily Wyatt

AMP&RSAND, INC.

Chicago • New Orleans

ISBN 978-099625250-8

Design
David Robson

Published by
AMPERSAND, INC.
515 Madison Street
New Orleans, Louisiana 70116

⸺

719 Clinton Place
River Forest, Illinois 60305

www.ampersandworks.com

Produced and Published in the United States
Printed in U.S.A.
22 21 20 19 18 17 16   2 3 4 5 6 7 8

To request a personalized copy or to schedule a book signing/school reading, email goodnightlittlerock@gmail.com

The author would like to thank the following, who allowed use of their images for reference:

Arkansas Department of Parks and Tourism
Skyline, Arkansas State Capitol, Rolling Hills

Paul Barrows
Pinnacle Mountain

Scott Head
River Market District

Little Rock Convention and Visitors Bureau
Little Rock Central High School National Historic Site, Arkansas Arts Center, Big Dam Bridge, Governors Mansion, River Market Trolley, Farmers Market, Clinton Presidential Center and Park, Witt Stephens, Jr. Central Arkansas Nature Center, War Memorial Stadium, Historic Arkansas Museum, Dickey-Stephens Park, Bridges, Downtown, Amphitheater

Museum of Discovery

Riverfest, Inc.

FOR PRESLEY AND LANDON

Goodnight Little Rock, the capital city
of The Natural State with places so pretty

Goodnight Pinnacle Mountain 1011 feet high

Goodnight tall pine trees that reach for the sky

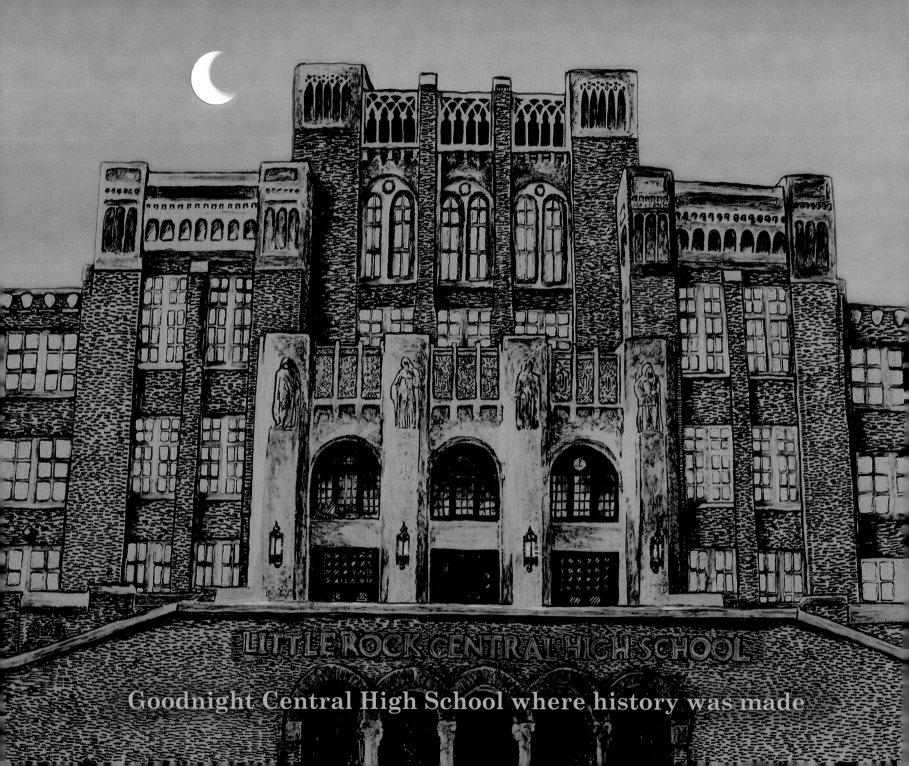

Goodnight Central High School where history was made

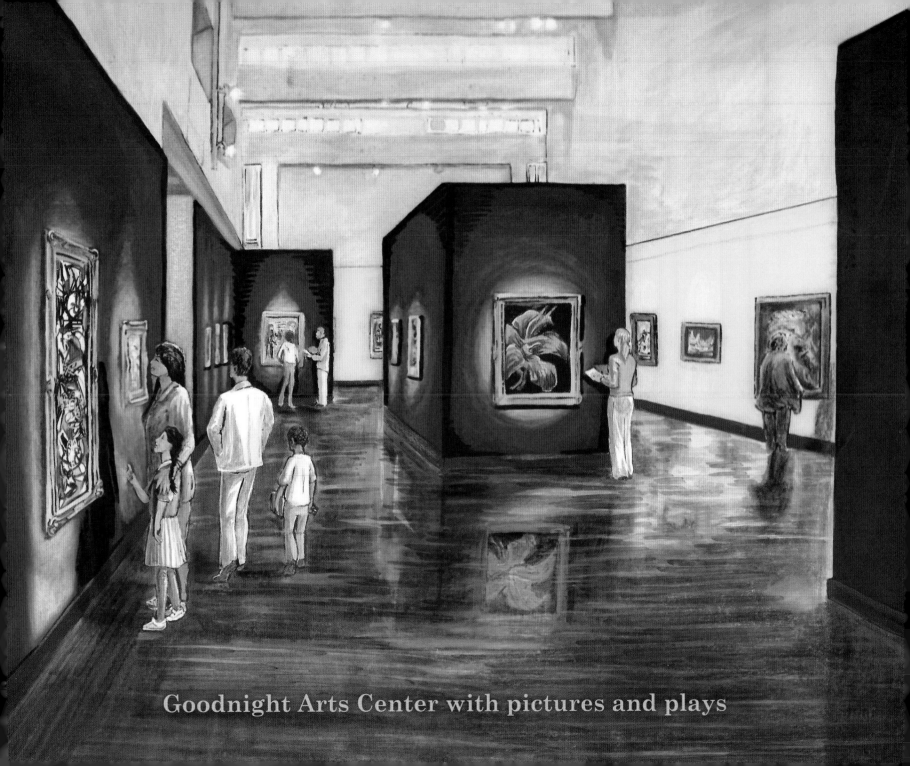

Goodnight Arts Center with pictures and plays

Goodnight Big Dam Bridge across the river so deep

Goodnight to the mansion where the Governor sleeps

Goodnight River Market and the trolleys that toot

Goodnight to the farmers selling veggies and fruit

Goodnight State Capitol and the work that is done

Goodnight Riverfest with music and fun

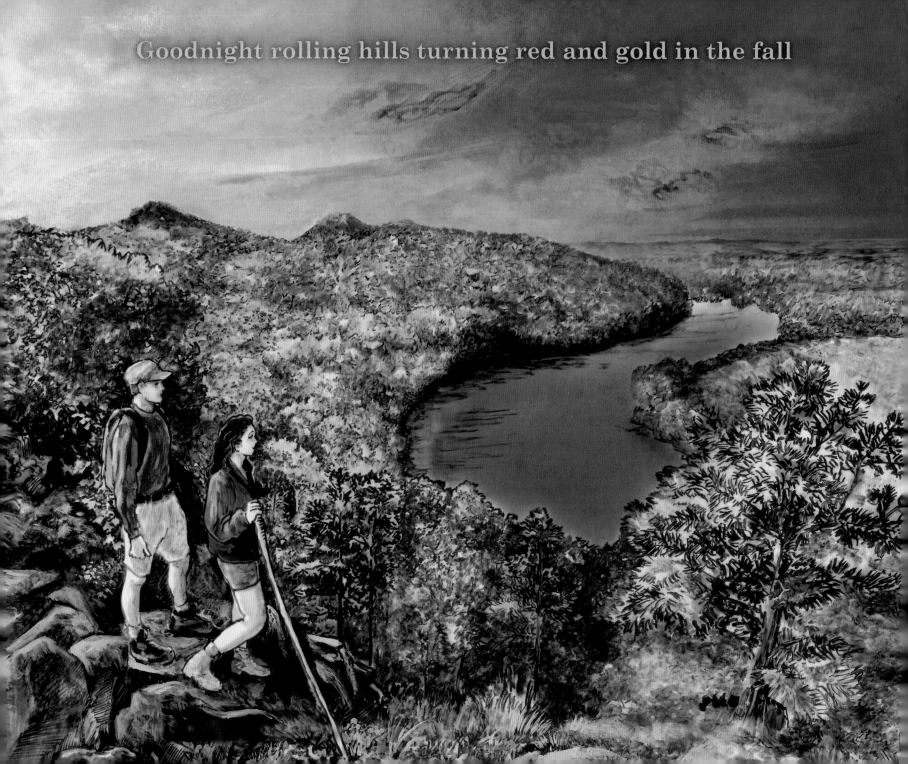
Goodnight rolling hills turning red and gold in the fall

Goodnight southern hospitality and friendly "hey y'alls"

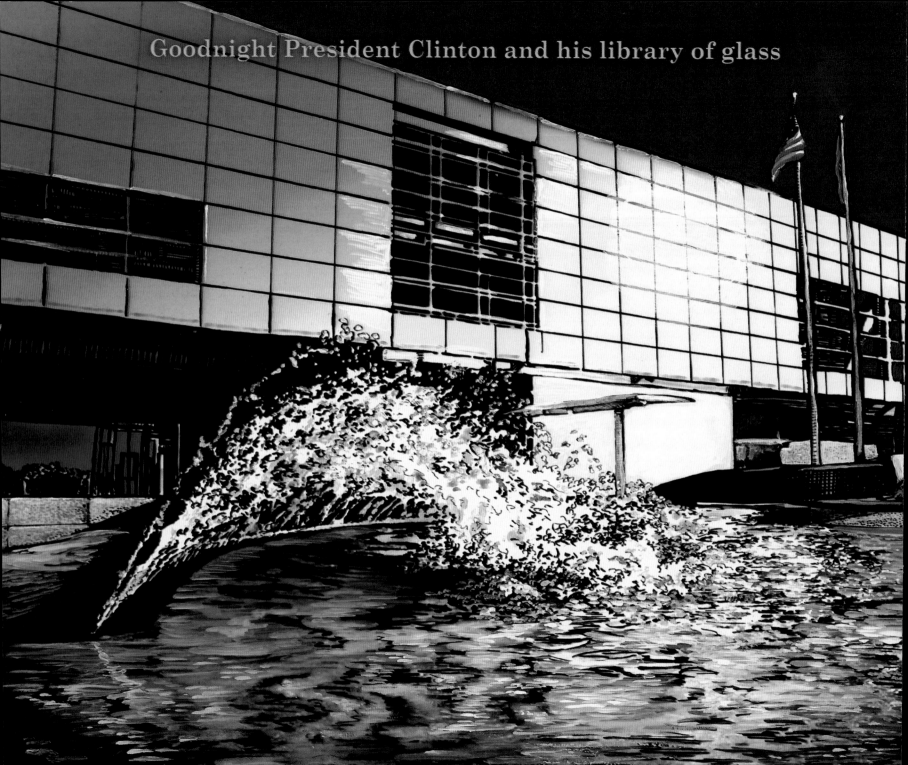

Goodnight President Clinton and his library of glass

Goodnight Nature Center with catfish and bass

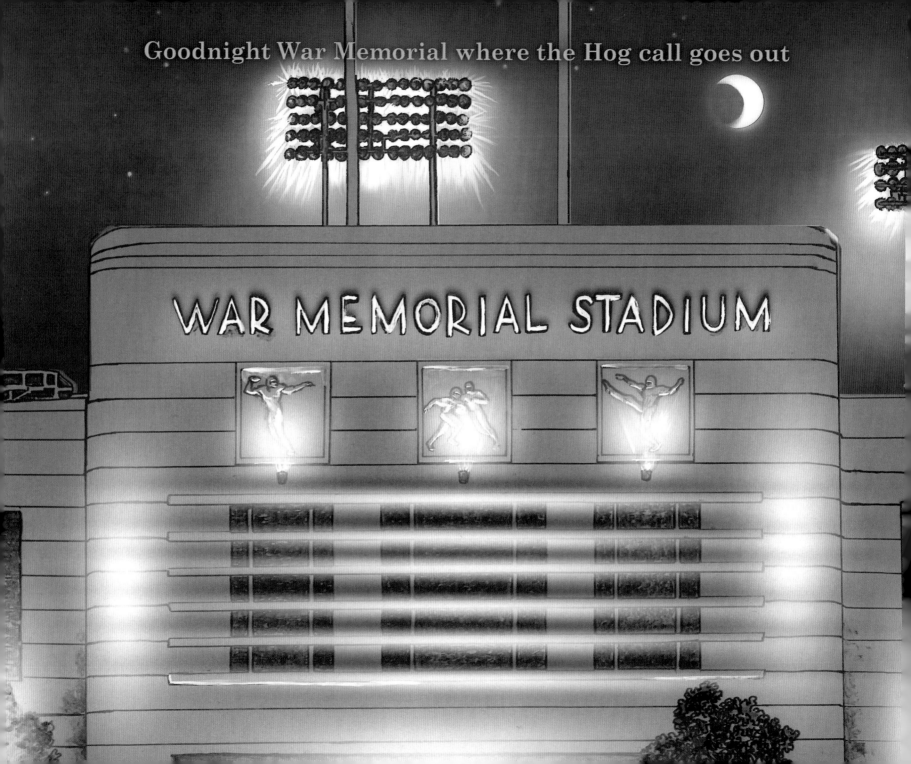

Goodnight War Memorial where the Hog call goes out

Goodnight Historic Arkansas Museum and Old Statehouse

Goodnight Museum of Discovery that makes learning such fun

Goodnight to the Travs and Dickey-Stephens Park

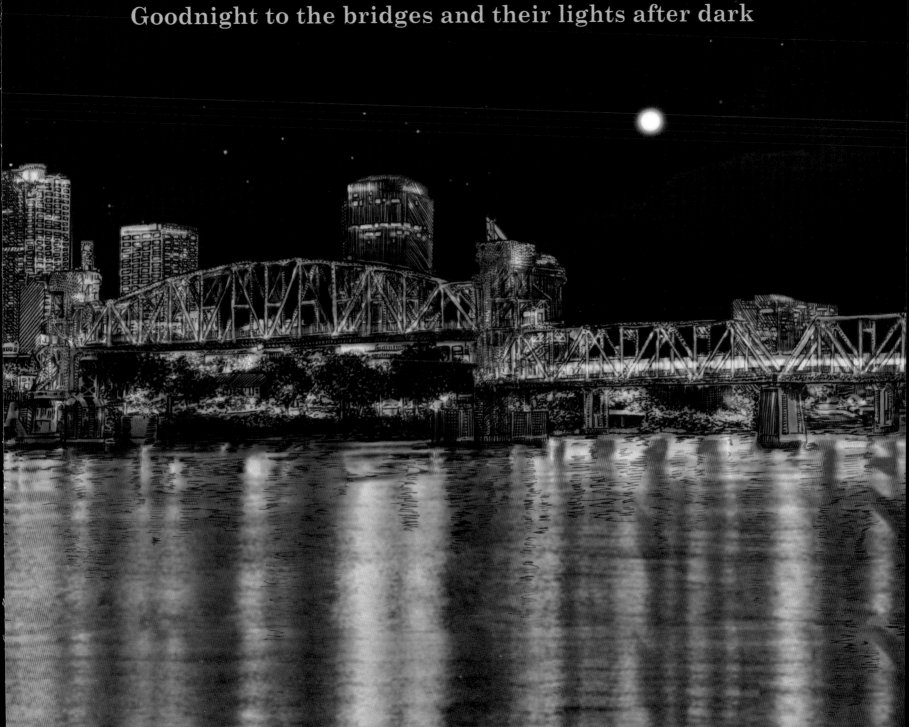

Goodnight to the bridges and their lights after dark

Goodnight downtown with restaurants and shops

Goodnight Amphitheater, the symphony and pops

Goodnight *La Petite Roche* as the early French explorers said
Goodnight Little Rock, it's time for bed

LITTLE ROCK GLOSSARY

LITTLE ROCK
Arkansas' state capital and largest city, Little Rock, was discovered in 1541 by Hernando De Soto. It was named *La Petite Roche* for the outcropping of rocks on the banks of the Arkansas River at the point where the rocks could be seen and used as a landmark for river travelers. www.littlerock.com

ARKANSAS RIVER
This major tributary of the Mississippi River starts in the Arkansas River Valley in Colorado. It stretches 1469 miles, and is the world's 45th longest river. It flows through Colorado, Kansas, Oklahoma and Arkansas. www.arkansasrivertrail.org

PINNACLE MOUNTAIN
Dedicated to preserving natural resources and providing environmental education, the Mountain has hiking and horse trails, and is Arkansas's first state park to be located near a major metropolitan area. www.arkansas stateparks.com/pinnaclemountain

LITTLE ROCK CENTRAL HIGH SCHOOL NATIONAL HISTORIC SITE
The school played an integral role in the 1957 desegregation crisis, as nine brave African-American students, "The Little Rock Nine," integrated the formerly all-white school. Central High is the nation's only functioning high school within the boundaries of a national historic site. www.nps.gov/chsc/index.htm

ARKANSAS ARTS CENTER
Opened in 1960, the Center is home to one of the state's leading cultural institutions with world-class exhibition galleries, the Arkansas Children's Theatre, a fine and performing arts school, sculpture courtyards and a reference library. The Center grew out of the Fine Arts Club of Arkansas, founded in 1914, and the Museum of Fine Arts, founded in 1937. www.arkarts.com

BIG DAM BRIDGE
Opened in 2006 atop Murray Lock & Dam, it is North America's longest pedestrian- and cyclist-intended bridge. It spans the Arkansas River, and serves as a link to the 17-mile Arkansas River Trail loop. www.bigdambridge.com

GOVERNOR'S MANSION
This is the official home of the people of Arkansas and their First Family. At one time the Arkansas School for the Blind was on this site. The Mansion is on the National Register of Historic Places. *Note*: The Mansion was a backdrop in the hit television series, "Designing Women." www.arkansasgovern orsmansion.com

RIVER MARKET DISTRICT
In downtown Little Rock, the District includes Ottenheimer Hall food vendors, art galleries, restaurants, shops, 33-acre Riverfront Park, public sculptures, entertainment and local music venues. www.rivermarket.info

RIVERFEST
This annual event is the state's largest festival, created in 1978 to celebrate the visual and performing arts. Held on the banks of the Arkansas River over Memorial Day weekend, the three-day festival draws more than 250,000 people each year. Some of the best names in music have performed at Riverfest. www.riverfestarkansas.com

ARKANSAS STATE CAPITOL
For more than 100 years, this neo-classical building has been known for its architectural excellence, having been designed after our nation's capitol building. It features multiple public memorials and is the heart of state government. The galleries are where the public can watch legislators at work. www.sos.arkansas.gov/stateCapitolInfo/ Pages/default.aspx

CLINTON PRESIDENTIAL CENTER AND PARK
The Clinton Presidential Center is the home of the Little Rock offices of the Clinton Foundation, the Clinton Presidential Library and Museum, and the Clinton School of Public Service. The Clinton Center is a world-class educational and cultural venue offering a variety of educational programs, special events, exhibitions, and lectures, presenting a unique perspective of the work—past, present, and future—of the 42nd President of the United States, William Jefferson Clinton. www.clintonpresidentialcenter.org

WITT STEPHENS, JR. CENTRAL ARKANSAS NATURE CENTER

Dedicated to restoring and maintaining Arkansas's fish and wildlife resources, the Center has live animals, an aquarium and interactive exhibits. **www.centralarkansas naturecenter.com**

WAR MEMORIAL STADIUM

The Stadium opened in 1948 following World War II. It was built as a tribute to those who served in World Wars I and II. Now it honors all Arkansans who have served and died for their country. The stadium is primarily used for football games, but is also a venue for special events. **www.wmstadium.com**

THE HOG CALL

Goes like this:

Woooooooo, Pig! Sooie!
Woooooooo, Pig! Sooie!
Woooooooo, Pig! Sooie! Razorbacks!

Calling the Hogs is a tradition of the University of Arkansas students, alumni and sports fans who add hand motions and fist pumps as they call.

HISTORIC ARKANSAS MUSEUM

Arkansas history and heritage are celebrated with historic home and grounds tours, living history characters, Arkansas-made exhibits, contemporary arts and an interactive children's gallery. **www.historicarkansas.org**

OLD STATE HOUSE MUSEUM

The Museum opened in 1836 and is the oldest standing state capitol west of the Mississippi River. It is dedicated to preserving the history of Arkansas from statehood onward. It served as the backdrop to President Clinton's 1992 and 1996 acceptance speeches. **www.oldstatehouse.com**

LITTLE ROCK ZOO

The Zoo opened in 1926 and houses more than 700 animals and 200 species. It features the Over-the-Jumps historic carousel and Arkansas Diamond Express train. At 33 acres, it is the largest zoo in Arkansas. **www.littlerockzoo.com**

MUSEUM OF DISCOVERY

Founded in 1927, Little Rock's oldest museum has been transformed to include 90 interactive exhibits and special programming designed to ignite a passion for science, technology, engineering and math. **www.museumofdiscovery.org**

THE TRAVS

This is one of the oldest nicknames in professional sports. The Arkansas Travelers, founded in 1901, is a charter member of professional baseball leagues. **arkansas.travelers.milb.com/index.jsp?sid=t574**

DICKEY-STEPHENS PARK

This Park was built in only 426 days and is home to the Arkansas Travelers. **arkansas. travelers.milb.com/index.jsp?sid=t574**

RIVER LIGHTS IN THE ROCK

Spanning the Arkansas River, three bridges—Main Street, Junction, and Clinton Presidential Park—are illuminated with millions of multi-colored L.E.D. lights providing nightly shows. **riverlightsintherock.com**

AMPHITHEATER

Located in the River Market's Riverfront Park along the Arkansas River, it is a top outdoor venue for concerts and events in Little Rock, including Riverfest. Current naming rights belong to First Security Bank. **www.rivermarket.info/learn-more/river fest-amphitheatre.aspx**

LA PETITE ROCHE

French for "the little rock," the city's namesake. Pieces of the rock are featured in La Petite Roche Place in Riverfront Park at the bottom of the Junction Bridge. The rock served as a landmark for early river travelers. **www.littlerock.com/things-to-do/detail/ la-petit-roche-plaza**

ABOUT THE AUTHOR
ABOUT THE ILLUSTRATOR

EMILY WYATT

Emily was born and raised in Little Rock. She graduated from the University of Central Arkansas with a degree in Business Administration. After living in Texas and New Mexico, Emily is happy to be back in her hometown with her family. Emily enjoys being outdoors. She has fond memories of camping and hiking throughout The Natural State. Pinnacle Mountain is one of her favorite places in Little Rock.

NATHANIEL DAILEY

Nathaniel began working professionally in fine art and illustration during college. He has sold work internationally in diverse styles and subject matter. His illustration work encompasses children's books, fiction, non-fiction, nature, fantasy, and album art. Nathaniel also teaches art at his studio based in Little Rock.